a pocketful of
RHYME

Imagination for a new generation

2006 Poetry Competition for 7-11 year-olds

YoungWriters

North Yorkshire
Edited by Michelle Afford

First published in Great Britain in 2007 by:
Young Writers
Remus House
Coltsfoot Drive
Peterborough
PE2 9JX
Telephone: 01733 890066
Website: www.youngwriters.co.uk

SB ISBN 1 84602 746 2

Foreword

Young Writers was established in 1991 and has been passionately devoted to the promotion of reading and writing in children and young adults ever since. The quest continues today. Young Writers remains as committed to the nurturing of poetic and literary talent as ever.

This year's Young Writers competition has proven as vibrant and dynamic as ever and we are delighted to present a showcase of the best poetry from across the UK and in some cases overseas. Each poem has been selected from a wealth of *A Pocketful Of Rhyme* entries before ultimately being published in this, our fourteenth primary school poetry series.

Once again, we have been supremely impressed by the overall quality of the entries we have received. The imagination, energy and creativity which has gone into each young writer's entry made choosing the poems a challenging and often difficult but ultimately hugely rewarding task - the general high standard of the work submitted ensured this opportunity to bring their poetry to a larger appreciative audience.

We sincerely hope you are pleased with this final collection and that you will enjoy *A Pocketful Of Rhyme North Yorkshire* for many years to come.

Contents

Celeste Mia Craggs (9)   18
Joshua Peacock (10)   19

Aysgarth School
Jack Williams-Ellis (9)   19
Humphrey Codrington   20
Alex Totty (9)   21
Hector Inglis (9)   22
Charlie I'Anson (9)   23
Edward Fenwick (9)   24
Mungo Blyth (9)   25
Mungo Fawcett (9)   26
Max Darbishire (9)   27
Alexander Onslow (9)   28

Carnagill CP School
Ranjeet Birbikram Shahi (11)   28
Ceara Lowe (9)   29
Lauren Horsfield (11)   29
Rachel Waters (9)   30
Rebecca Cooper (10)   30
Adam Senior (10)   30
Khalian Deighton (9)   31
Jade Mills (11)   31
Connour Taylor (10)   31
Emma Humphryson (9)   32
Courtney Wooldridge (9)   32
Daniel Dickinson (11)   32
Chloe Goult (10)   33

Follifoot CE Primary School
Liam Auty (10)   33
Millie Isaacson (9)   34
William Caldecott (9)   34
Ben Goddard (9)   35
Daniel Walker (10)   35
Isabelle Lee (9)   36
Benjamin Ball (9)   37
Sophie Webster (9)   38
Charlotte Preston (9)   39
Laura Summersall (10)   40

Osmotherley CP School

Ellie Hore (8)	55
Sam Liburd (8)	55
Sally Hughlock (10)	55
Liam Turner (10)	56
Nick Foxton (10)	56
James Marriott (11)	57
Nathan Adam Wood (7)	57
Esther Torniley-Walker (10)	58
Joseph Wood (10)	58
Harry Brass (10)	59
William Marriott (7)	59
Joe Allison (10)	60
William Stamp (10)	60

St Mary's Primary School, Knaresborough

Megan Eustace (10)	61
Nicola Milligan (9)	61
Patrick Sunley (9)	62
Jordan Firth (9)	62
Thomas Brennan (9)	63
Jacob Fincham Dukes (9)	63
Eleanor Churchill (9)	64
Louie Barker (9)	64
Adena Keeys (9)	65
Libby Owens (10)	65

St Mary's RC Primary School, Selby

Rachel Jackson (9)	66
Ruby Waterworth (9)	66
Beth Keeble (9)	66
Shannon Nee (10)	67
Chloe Grundy (11)	67
Amy Grundy (10)	67
Hannah Savage (10)	68
Hayley Dalrymple (10)	68
Jamie Graley (9)	68
Niall Sullivan & Malachi Brown (8)	69
Philippa Clay (8)	69
Nicole Hey (8)	69
Gabrielle Cooke (8)	70

Sean Corrigan (8)   70
Kellie Nee (9)   71
Niall Coulthard (8)   71
Alex Keeble (9)   72

Spofforth CE Primary School
Katie Bruce (11)   72
Katie Booth (9)   73
Charlotte Freeman (10)   73
Christopher Horne (10)   74
Nicholas Honey (10)   75
Joe Horne (9)   75
Samuel Goddard (10)   76
Thomas Goldring (10)   76
Damon Hammond (9)   77

Woodthorpe Primary School
Tobias Mitchell (9)   77
Chloe Fletcher (9)   78
Erin Morgan (7)   78
Tony Fowler (10)   79
Cameron Loftus (7)   79
Amy Martyn (10)   80
Natasha Askew (9)   80
Thomas Murden (9)   81
Jordan Bryszkiewski (7)   81
Alex Frasina (9)   82
Chloe Robertson (8)   82
Robert Smith (9)   83
Natasha Healey (9)   83
Amy Rowlinson (10)   84
Ella Duke (7)   84
Jack Allinson (9)   85
Megan Brittain (8)   85
Declan Barnett (9)   86
Chloe Muggeridge (7)   86
Thomas Pannet (9)   87
Daniel Corr (7)   87
Michelle Dupley (9)   88
Naomi Martyn (7)   88
Kayley Bayston (9)   89

Shumi Miah (11)	89
Zach Dodson (8)	90
Billy Hayes (9)	90
Declan Horncastle (9)	91
Chloe Fletcher (9)	91
Alex Fowler (10)	92
Becky Muggeridge (7)	92
Jessica Cheung (9)	93
Rebekah Moore (9)	93
Thomas Ibbott (7)	94
Chelsea Richardson (7)	94
James Smith (7)	95
Lewis Fletcher (7)	95
Keelie Mollan (9)	96
Matthew Chaplin (9)	96
Amy Louise Martin (10)	97
Evan Morris (7)	97
Jack Hughes (7)	98
Georgia Muir (7)	98
Emily Henman (10)	99
Rebecca Jakes (8)	99
Benjamin Lacey (9)	100
Amy Milne (9)	100
Charley Preston (9)	101
Jordan Smith (10)	101
Adam Saun (9)	102
Harry Ford (10)	102
Dylan Howlett (9)	103
Jamal Ahmed (10)	103
Emily Smith (9)	104
Benjamin Acey (10)	104
Danielle Hickman (9)	105
Chloe Richardson (8)	105
Stephanie Watmough (10)	106
Luke Wilson (10)	106
James Chapman & Mapalo (8)	107
Lauren Stewart (10)	107
Hannah Brown (10)	108
Anna Sibley (10)	108
Joseph Devonport (10)	109
Vicki Hall (10)	109
Jennifer Tompkins (10)	110

The Poems

The Golden Dragon

There was once a dragon called Nettlebrand,
Who roamed around the streets
He had shiny golden armour
And sheep and goats were the only things he ate,
He had a servant called Twiglegs,
Who was as small as a dwarf,
And one weird thing about Twiglegs was that when he went to sleep,
He hung himself on the ceiling, using loads of pegs,
And one thing about Nettlebrand was that when he went to sleep,
He did drown in the water,
To where it was very deep!

Reece Ingham (9)

The Storm Is A Snake

The storm is a snake
Darting at you
Ready to attack at any time
Its forked tongue, deadly and red
So that makes the snake one of the bad

It waits silent and quiet until . . .
It pounces so fast!
It sinks its fangs into its prey which now lives in the past
It hisses while crashing into the rocks
If you are near you don't want to stay!

But on days like in May and June
The snake stops and very soon
It stops hissing too
Everything becomes silent once again.

Joel Tankard (10)
Amotherby Community Primary School

My Big Sister

My big sister, Nicky,
Is sometimes very tricky.
Most of the time she's busy,
But the rest of the time she's dizzy.

She has a boyfriend called Paul,
But she drives me up the wall.
She tells me what to do,
When she hasn't got a clue.

But when I'm feeling sad and down,
She wipes away that bad old frown.
She is a very good big sister,
When she's gone, I really miss her.

Kirstie Allen (9)
Amotherby Community Primary School

Sam The Pony

Sam the pony went for a ride
Down the lane with a hedge either side
A blackbird suddenly, out it flew
I fell off and landed in poo.

Oh dear, I think I stink,
Better go home and jump in the sink.

Scrub, scrub, scrub been in the tub
Now I'm clean, fit to be seen.

Back in the stable Sam's bushy
And bright so I turn off the light
And wish him goodnight.

Charlotte Hoggard (9)
Amotherby Community Primary School

My Friends

When Dan and Alex came to play
We messed about in mud and clay
We played with my dog
When we came across a frog
We rode our bikes about
Then I heard my mum shout out
All you could hear was us munch lunch, 'Lunch!'
She made us all go for a walk
By gum, we do like to talk
Hurry up, she says
We're too set in our ways
We have to say, we're only nine
And life is just fine.

Jack Illingworth (9)
Amotherby Community Primary School

My Dogs

I have a dog called Pippin,
He's small, furry and white,
He's especially fond of chicken,
And he licks my face in the night.

I have a dog called Bridget,
She likes chicken too,
All she ever does is fidget,
And not what I tell her to.

Murphy is my other dog,
He's very, very tall,
He likes to jump, he likes to jog,
But he sleeps most of all.

Zoe Hume (9)
Amotherby Community Primary School

A Family Baby Boom

You may be surprised, you may not
But guess what, we had a baby boom in our family
It all started off with my cousin Kate
She told us she was pregnant and the baby came late
A girl named Abbie
Then it was my cousin Lisa, she had a baby boy
And the baby did please her
A boy named Isaac

After, it was my cousin Diane
She had a baby girl
Who had a little curl
A girl named Ella
Next it was my cousin, Vicki
She had twins
That really wins
Two girls named Erin and Grace

And not that long ago we found out . . .
What could it be about?
That my cousin Lisa's pregnant again
Will it be Jack or a Jane
Or a boom, boom, boom
One of each
Maybe triplets too
Jane, Jack and Marylou

Baby boom!

Ria Williams (9)
Amotherby Community Primary School

Tiger

T errifying teeth, saliva dripping!
I cy looks as he gets ready to steal his prey
G rowling as he prowls through the long grass
E erie eyes darting about
R eady paws waiting to gasp his prey . . .

Hannah Poole (9)
Amotherby Community Primary School

The Scorpion

The scorpion, a howling lion,
With its pincers swishing like iron,
As it pierces like steel,
The pain you can feel,
As it attacks its prey,
And silence is all it can say . . .

The cold-blooded beast walks with pride,
As all the animals stay one side,
Its scary stinger swishing in fear,
Its swishing and slashing is all you can hear,
A ruler with power, peace and glory,
And that's an amazing scorpion story . . .

Its stunning red armour which protects,
From the great predatorial giant insects,
With its poisonous kill,
Which turns all enemies still,
As the storming lion hunts,
For its pride as it stunts . . .

It is like an angry storm,
With its rivals torn,
As anger comes irate,
And the humans it can hate,
As the scorpion roars like a lord of beasts,
And all non-allies are its feasts.

Jonathan Pitkin (10)
Amotherby Community Primary School

Hamsters

I like hamsters,
They sleep all day,
When it's night-time,
They come out to play.

Sarah Wakefield (9)
Amotherby Community Primary School

Dieting Is A Riot

Guess what, I'm going on a diet,
Argh, it's going to be a riot.

I tried going swimming,
I did try skimming.

I'm going to be a dude, a queen of healthy food!

I know, I will try skipping,
I ate some mushrooms, I started gipping

All I want to do is watch my telly,
But I've got to concentrate on my belly.

I'm really wealthy,
But I'm not healthy.

If I go on a walk,
I always try to talk.

I like to be funny,
Hop round like a bunny.

I've got a disgusting habit,
I'd like to be a rabbit.

Because they're healthy but they're not wealthy!

Yeah.

Megan Shaw (9)
Amotherby Community Primary School

Acrostic - Lion

L ying about all day long.
I n the shade of an old oak tree.
O n the grass, lying down.
N aughty and fierce for killing animals.

Jacob Pilmer (9)
Amotherby Community Primary School

An Angry Storm

A storm is anger about to start,
You feel the pain coming straight from the heart.
The thunder is a voice, loud it may seem,
A roar, a shout and then a scream.

The storm, it spreads and it can fly,
Like a teardrop coming down from the eye.
It slaps its victim, a lightning strike,
There are very few things storms tend to like.

The sky turns black almost everywhere,
It's a very dark mood flowing through the air.
The rain starts pouring down from the sky,
It's gotten so angry it begins to cry.

You may be safe inside the house,
But outside, you're no safer than a mouse.
Quickly, quickly, run inside,
It's the only place you can hide.

It's lightning there and lightning here,
Careful it doesn't get too near.
The storm slowly, slowly grows,
Where will it strike next? Who knows, who knows!

Jodie Caston (10)
Amotherby Community Primary School

Everton

E xcellent team scoring goals!
V ery evil rivals (Liverpool).
E lectric fans eating sausage rolls.
R ivals for Everton drool.
T raining is on the way.
O n the way to becoming cool!
N ever miss 'Match of the Day'.

Evan Tankard (9)
Amotherby Community Primary School

My Hamster

My hamster, in her cage, went round and round,
She hardly came to the ground.
She came for feed-time, of course she would,
She came out with an awful thud.

Then suddenly you heard her wheel again,
Surely, by now she feels a pain.
But no, my hamster kept on going,
When she would stop there was no knowing.

But one day she escaped from her cage,
My mum let out an awful rage,
She thought she would be in the cupboard,
But if she was or not I was not bothered.

What all that spinning was for,
Was just to open the cage door,
My hamster is really clever,
If you thought she was dumb, you could say it never!

I decided to watch the telly,
It could get rid of my mood cold and grey.
There was a programme about animals on,
It said breeding season started yesterday.

So my hamster must have been looking
For a mate somewhere around,
Oh I hoped she knew,
Where my house was found.

The next day she was back again, thankfully,
But she wasn't in her wheel
Because pregnant was she.

Ailsa Anson (9)
Amotherby Community Primary School

The Storm Is A Shark

The storm is a shark, bloodthirsty and wild,
Cunning, scary and freaky.
Floating along, luring its prey,
So naughty and so sneaky.
Making such a scary sound,
Big and bad like a fox.
Lashing out gold thunder,
Beating all the cliff rocks.

People running one by one,
Away from this terrible sin.
One fell over and was caught by the storm,
Must have drunk too much gin.
As mad and as bad as a spinning tornado,
Breaking everything in its way.
Zooming around, this way and that,
Lasting all night and all day.

Making a mess, blowing things around,
Like crisp packets and an empty Coke can.
Nothing can defeat the storm, it even sends,
A shiver down the spine of a man.

I'm coming to the end of my story,
Standing in all its glory.
I hope that you've enjoyed it and you'll come back some day,
The storm might come again and it might blow you away!

Declan Gough (10)
Amotherby Community Primary School

My Cat, Mickey

M ade to play
 I rresistibly cute and cuddly
C lever and curious
K aleidoscope of colours
E nemy of the mouse
Y ou'd better be ready for Mickey.

David Joshua Horne (10)
Amotherby Community Primary School

The Volcano

The storm is a strong volcano,
Dark as the black cloud,
Bubbling up its vicious waves,
Roaring out its destruction.

Fierce eruptions will kill,
Pounding all the people with its waves,
Bloodthirsty monster attacks,
Crashing and bashing, the monster is angry.

Suddenly, the monster goes to sleep,
Everything slows down, no more destruction.
All is calm.

Isaac Johnson (10)
Amotherby Community Primary School

The Hyena

A storm is a hyena,
Murderous and fast,
Destroying everything in its path,
Whilst striking its lightning,
It makes dying fast.

Its teeth so strong, so thick,
Its power is undoubtable,
Its calling strikes fear,
To anything near,
It's thunder when it's roaring.

It calmly rests,
The rain stops,
But anything near is still wary,
Of its presence.

William Spencer (10)
Amotherby Community Primary School

The Storm Is A Lion

The storm is lion thundering with his tail,
He pounces on his victim.
He eats, then roars,
He sits licking his paws.
He stands on a giant thorn,
The rain is his tears,
His skin is torn.
But his dark mood soon shows.
People run away as his anger grows.
He is frightening as he thunders past the crowd.
He clashes a large beam of lightning.
He roars again.
Thunder and lightning crash all over until everything goes silent.
The lion is asleep.

Ellen Clayton (10)
Amotherby Community Primary School

My Cat, Smokie

My cat, Smokie, is very fat.
I suppose she's a very big cat.

Lazing here, lazing there,
Lazing just everywhere.

The car goes beep,
She's asleep.
She gets woken up,
And the birds go *cheep!*

So now you know my cat, Smokie, is very fat!

Sophie Floris (10)
Amotherby Community Primary School

The Snake

The storm is a fierce snake,
Slithering all over the place, hissing and pouncing.
Its teeth jamming over the ground like lightning,
It makes movements like a snake waiting to attack.

The storm is calming down now,
The snake has grabbed its prey.
Its hissing getting quieter and quieter,
Its caught his prey, moaning,
It's calming down, slithering away back into darkness.

The storm has gone like a snake calming down,
Hiding in the darkness, waiting to pounce on its next victim,
The predator waiting to kill its victim with its poisonous teeth,
Like the lightning flashing, like the snake on its prey.

Max Fraser (10)
Amotherby Community Primary School

My Little Brother!

My little brother goes to school with me,
He's always annoying and he bothers me.

When I am tired
He goes all wild!

I am 5 years older
And he's only a child.

When he's older he'll
Be just like me!

Rosie Hannah Roberts (9)
Amotherby Community Primary School

The Storm Is Like A Lion

The storm is a lion who roars at first, trying to cause some trouble.
He waits to pounce,
While the rain comes down and bounces on the road.

While brewing he roars in his dark mood.
He darts, he snarls out in the rain.
When he revs up he tears houses down,
Like an eating victim.

He paws and grabs while trying to calm down.
Then there is suddenly a roar,
Now there is no more,
Apart from the spitting rain.

Alexandra Ennis (10)
Amotherby Community Primary School

Dinosaurs

It crashes in
with a mighty roar
and in front of me
I see a dinosaur.

Its lumpy back
and scary roar,
I hear its footsteps
on the floor.

You hear a noise
they begin to scatter,
I'm left wondering
what's the matter?

David Goode (9)
Amotherby Community Primary School

Anger

A storm is creeping anger,
Creeping, crawling, shouting boo,
Now revving up,
Harder and harder,
Sneaking, sneaking up on you!

Fierce, scary, darkened mood,
Tears start tripping down and down,
Cowering away,
Don't want to meet it again,
Your heart going *pound, pound*

Calming, calming, calming down,
Relaxed, relaxed, dying down,
Whispering, whirling, curling no more,
Can hear nothing in the air.

Sara Pycock (10)
Amotherby Community Primary School

The Lion

The storm is a roaring lion
The storm is a killing lion
Breaking through the trees
Pounding, pounding for attack
Clashing in the stormy wind
Lightning as fast as darts
The loud thunder is as loud as roaring
The crackling of lightning is like lions eating bones
The rain falls down, scaring people
Flashing down as a scary lion.

Henry Bulmer (10)
Amotherby Community Primary School

The Roaring Lion

The storm is a roaring lion
Brewing calmly and sneakily
It clashes, waiting to pounce
Revving up in its dark gloomy mood.

It roars loudly, grabbing his victim
Pouncing, running fiercely through the long grass
Its big black paws making footprints as it plods along.

The roaring lion walks home slowly
Watching for more victims
It settles down
For the long, dark, stormy night ahead.

Hannah Hopkin (10)
Amotherby Community Primary School

The Storm

The storm is a fierce lion,
It creeps up on its prey,
The wind is its growl,
The thump of its paws is the thunder.

Lightning strikes when its paw swipes,
Caught with a prick of lightning,
The deer moans but the lion roars,
He chews and the wind roars.

The lion falls asleep,
Its snoring is the thunder,
It moves along to another place,
You never hear a peep.

Sophie Miller (10)
Amotherby Community Primary School

My Naughty Kittens

K is for kitten, trying to catch a butterfly.
I is for it's time to play.
T is for two thirsty kittens lapping up milk.
T is for time to curl up and sleep.
E is for eating tuna.
N is for naughty little playful kittens.

Victoria Boyes (9)
Amotherby Community Primary School

The Storm

The storm's my mum in anger
She shouts at me with rage

Lightning hurts your eyes
Thunder hurts your ears

She revs up in fury
She cools down in happiness

She wears a zigzag face
Just like the lightning wears.

Helen Craggs (10)
Amotherby Community Primary School

Monster Poem

The lightest door,
leads to the darkest room
and in the darkest room
there's the darkest face
and then . . .
Snap!

Isobel Kerins (9)
Amotherby Community Primary School

Snakes

The waves are a poisonous bite,
The rain hisses from the sky.
The wind is a slither through the air,
It attacks the animals and people there.

They do not care!

Frightening sounds that send shivers down your spine,
It lets out a little whine and then it stays still all the time.

They do not care!

Anna Donkin (10)
Amotherby Community Primary School

Wild Horses

The storm is a wild horse,
Rearing and bucking of course,
He's wild like the wind,
The big victim is pinned.

He takes two steps back then he lashes out,
The victim takes his pride off the field,
The hunter has failed to take the pride of the wild horse.

Cameron Hardie (10)
Amotherby Community Primary School

The Storm

The storm roars when it dashes,
It brings tears to your lashes,
Fear to your laughter.
It brings shivers to your spine,
As frightening as it can be,
Stay still in fright and fear.

Shona Young (10)
Amotherby Community Primary School

Football Crazy

I'm football crazy
I'm football mad,
When I scored a goal
My mum was really glad.

When I went to training
I scored another goal,
My dad was really happy
And he brought me a foal.

At half-time
We were up one-nil,
My coach was delighted
His name was Phil.

At the end of the season
We came first,
Everyone was happy
They looked like they would burst.

So I'm football crazy
I'm football mad!

Callum Smith (9)
Amotherby Community Primary School

Summer Fun In The Sun

In the salty sea, *swish, swish*
Sunbathing in the scorching hot sun
Ice cream melting in the red-hot, glowing sun
Children laughing and having fun in the sun
Making sandcastles on the sparkling hot sand
So we all love the sun in the summertime.

Celeste Mia Craggs (9)
Amotherby Community Primary School

Storm

The storm is a fierce, roaring lion
The storm is a killer, a bloodthirsty predator
Looking sweet and cute
But underneath, a vicious killer

It growls and prowls and all things else
Attacking its prey
Digging its claws, tearing the flesh off your bones
Attacking its prey, eating them whole

When the damage is done
It heads for the shade
And closes its eyes
And sleeps for the day

Joshua Peacock (10)
Amotherby Community Primary School

Happy

You're as happy
as a dog going home
as a mermaid with a comb
as a child in the sunshine
as a gourmet going to dine

You're as happy
as a sunflower in the light
as a photographer who saw a great sight
as a Frenchman drinking wine
as a star about to shine

You're as happy
as a teacher with no work to mark
as a spirit in the dark
as a sportsman who's on TV
as a man who just found a diamond key.

Jack Williams-Ellis (9)
Aysgarth School

Happy

You're as happy
As the golden sun
As an Aysgarth boy with his prep done
As a cub with his first prey
As a bride on her wedding day

You're as happy
As an angler with a mammoth trout
As a Christmas dinner without a single sprout
As a child given a new pup
As England winning the World Cup

You're as happy
As a robber with some money
As a bee with the most honey
As a teacher on his half day
As a boy on his eighth birthday

You're as happy
As a just-fed snake
As a schoolboy at break
As the moon at night
As a child flying a kite.

Humphrey Codrington
Aysgarth School

Sadness

You're as sad
as a world without peace
as a robber caught by the police
as a child without parents
as a group owing rent

You're as sad
as a dog with no home
as a mermaid who lost her comb
as a boy with a dead pup
as a footballer who lost the World Cup

You're as sad
as a man who lost his wife
as a child who lost their life
as a girl without a mobile phone
as a singer who lost their tone

You're as sad
as an Aysgarth boy with extra prep
as a dancer who can't master a step
as toy that is not used
as a Muslim wrongly accused.

Alex Totty (9)
Aysgarth School

Happy

You're as happy
as a boy with a birthday in May,
as a bride on her wedding day,
as a boy on half term,
as a brat killing a worm.

As happy
as a thief with lots of gold,
as a princess with a knight so bold,
as a teacher on her half day,
as a boy catching a ray.

As happy
as a boy winning a cup,
as a girl getting a pup,
as a hunter shooting a duck,
as a girl with good luck.

As happy
as a boy finding a website called bbc.co.uk,
as a boy that won croquet,
as a boy in the news,
as a man that sold his ewes.

As happy
as an astronaut going to space,
as a man winning a race,
as a boy at break,
as a man holding a snake.

Hector Inglis (9)
Aysgarth School

Happy

You're as happy
as a boy on his birthday
as a teacher on her half day
as a drunk lady
as a mother of a newborn baby

You're as happy
as a golf fan given an autograph by Tiger Woods
as a boy having jam tart for puds
as a dog with a bone
as a tramp given a home

You're as happy
as a lady on her wedding day
as a boy going to a birthday
as a girl with a new mobile phone
as a husband with a wife that doesn't moan

You're as happy
as a man that just became a millionaire
as a boy that got a girlfriend because of his hair
as a girl finding a new studying website called bbc.co.uk
as a women given a bouquet

You're as happy
as Europe winning the Ryder Cup
as a child given a pup
as a man on top of the world
as a cat, warm and curled.

Charlie l'Anson (9)
Aysgarth School

Quiet

You're as quiet
as a lion looking for its prey
as a teacher at the end of the day
as a boy eating his tuck
as a cooking roast duck

As quiet
as a bird without his beak
as a telltale classroom sneak
as a newborn pup
as an auctioneer looking at an ancient cup

As quiet
as a small gush of wind
as a vocal chord been pinged
as a boy in the corner of the room
as a ghost in a tomb

As quiet
as penalties in the World Cup
as a balloonist, way up
as a rabbit sitting
as a grandma knitting

You're nearly as quiet as me!

Edward Fenwick (9)
Aysgarth School

Lonely

You're as lonely as a baby with no mum
as a pupil who can't answer a sum
as a child who hasn't a birthday
as a boy who can't say

You're as lonely as a boy in a coma
as a boy who can't do karate
as a boy without a game
as a boy who can't be slain

You're as lonely as a prisoner with no hope of release
as a boy who is a beast
as the only boy not slain by evil men
as a boy who was dumped by his girlfriend, Jen

You're as lonely as a tramp
as a man who didn't make the skateboard ramp
as a boy lost in the park
as a boy alive in a shark

You're as lonely as the last turkey on the shelf
as a child running out of health
as a baby left in a house with the door locked
as a mum with her baby's head chopped.

Mungo Blyth (9)
Aysgarth School

Proud

You're as proud
As a lion with freshly shampooed hair
As a guy that got a hole-in-one and became a millionaire
As a super-speedy tennis ace that won the open cup
As a swirly free kick that beat the Bradford Pups

You're as proud
As a rhyme that works really well
As a girl in a five-star hotel
As a boy that scored his hat-trick
As a man that learnt a new kick

You're as proud
As a newly made president
As a dad that gave the best present
As a man that's in the England squad
As a farmer that bought a new quad

You're as proud
As a turtle with a shiny shell
As a shop that made a record sell
As a man that became the Holy Pope
As a newly made telescope

You're as proud
As a lioness with a lion
As a cleaner with an iron
As boy with a trial for Liverpool
As a boy that swam 200 lengths and became really cool.

Mungo Fawcett (9)
Aysgarth School

Happy

You're as happy
as a bird being freed from its cage
as a man who survived the Ice Age
as a dog with a bone
as the Queen with the throne

You're as happy
as a women who's got a furry coat
as a man who's got a new boat
as a boy with a toy
as a girl with a boy

You're as happy
as a robber who stole some money
as a bee with some honey
as a groom with a huge wedding day
as a king that had a speech to say

You're as happy
as a cricketer who made a good catch
as a coach when one of his players has won the cricket match
as a hunter that has got a new gun
as a boy having fun

You're as happy
as a priest that did God's wish
as an angler who caught his first fish
as England winning the World Cup
as a boy getting a new pup.

Max Darbishire (9)
Aysgarth School

Slow

You're as slow
as a thirty-year-old dog
as a fat warthog
as a crawling snail
as old style mail.

You're as slow
as the oldest granny in the world
as a person getting up when he is curled
as the time passing before Christmas Day
as the journey to Bramcote, such a long way.

You're as slow
as a wiggling worm
as the long summer term
as it is for a newborn baby to learn.

Alexander Onslow (9)
Aysgarth School

Water

Water in the ocean
Water in the sea
Water in the river
You can't catch me
Water is so precious
Life depends on it
Your mum uses it to wash your PE kit
Water in the ocean
Water in the sea
Water in the canyon
You surround me.

Ranjeet Birbikram Shahi (11)
Carnagill CP School

Horses

Horses are kind, horses are gentle.
They don't like my brother, because my brother is mental!
Sitting in the saddle, high up in the air.
While all the other horses just stand and stare.
Dads watching, waiting until they can praise us.
Oh no, Toby's bucked and, oh my goodness she's landed in poo.
You're hoping it won't happen to you.
Going so fast my hair is dancing,
While Flynn is wonderfully prancing.
Flynn so tall, so cute with his long black mane and tail.
With such a horse you cannot fail.
As beautiful as they are, I wish for one upon a shooting star.

Ceara Lowe (9)
Carnagill CP School

Magical Differences

There are a lot of differences between a witch and a fairy,
To start off with, a witch is hairy,
They walk around with their heads up high,
And kick you hard as you walk by,
Their hats may look like a big black cone,
But be aware, they'll turn you to stone!

But when it comes to a fairy,
They're not all that scary,
They have little wings,
And when they fly they make tiny tings,
They wave their wand,
And wish for a pond,
So this is the difference between a witch and a fairy.

Lauren Horsfield (11)
Carnagill CP School

Weird And Wonderful Creatures

Pixies are witty
When speaking to witches
Dragons and fairies
Are very caring
Grass bangers, scab scratchers
Are magical to see
In the world there are weird and wonderful creatures!

Rachel Waters (9)
Carnagill CP School

A Poem About Me

My hair is shiny as silk,
My eyes are as blue as the fresh sea,
My eyelashes are like a hairy gorilla,
My nose is as smooth as the table,
My lips are as pink as a rose,
My freckles are as orange as an orange,
My behaviour is as bad as a brat,
Now you know all about me.

Rebecca Cooper (10)
Carnagill CP School

The Monster

Very scary
Very hairy
But who is it?
Very cheeky
Very freaky
But who is it?
Very spotty
Very knotty
But who is it?
It's the monster!

Adam Senior (10)
Carnagill CP School

Mysterious Creatures In The Dark

Dancing shadows in the dark,
I am scared that there's a monster,
Here comes a dragon with his green scales and fiery-red wings,
What is he doing? He's using my phone,
Now he's looking at me with his sharp teeth and here are his
                                        mysterious friends,

One is a T-rex with blood on his teeth,
Now I am scared, it's dark in my room,
What is this? It's my mum calling me,
Phew! It's over and I am going to school.

Khalian Deighton (9)
Carnagill CP School

Teachers

Good things about teachers!

T is for true
E is for they give us education
A is for angel
C is for caring
H is for happy
E is for excellent
R is for reliable
S is for smile.

Jade Mills (11)
Carnagill CP School

A Poem About Me

My hair is as brown as a monkey.
My eyes shine like diamonds.
My skin is as fine as porcelain.
And my ears are as big as my finger.
My feet are as smelly as a dog.

Connour Taylor (10)
Carnagill CP School

I Would Like To Be. . .

I would like to be a diver,
And swim in the soggy sea,
Or perhaps a hairdresser,
That's maybe better for me,
Next I will be Super Girl,
And save all the kings.
Then I'll make sure that I have see-through wings.
But that's all in my dreams,
Maybe they will come true!

Emma Humphryson (9)
Carnagill CP School

Hallowe'en

Tonight on Hallowe'en
The darkness comes out
Children flash their torches
If you're a vampire
Go home when the sun rises
Nobody must find out about you
But if they do
You must suck their blood!

Courtney Wooldridge (9)
Carnagill CP School

I Wish

I wish upon a star,
I wish for something new.
I wish upon a snowflake,
That falls down on you.

I wish I had a million pounds,
I'd go abroad and admire the view.
I'd spend my money in expensive shops,
And go and visit Aunty Lou.

Daniel Dickinson (11)
Carnagill CP School

All About Me

My hair is as long as a door.
My ears are as thin as bars.
My skin is as hard as hard stones.
And my eyes are as round as Mars.
My toes are as brown as a tree trunk.
My nose is as pointy as a thorn.
My legs are as big as bricks.
And my arms are the same size as prawns.
My eyebrows are as smooth as a screen.
My hands are as small as a stone.
My neck is as clean as a new table.
And my lips don't have a single bone.
My body is a bit silly.
My feet are as nice as flowers.
My mouth is as big as a tower.
And my real name is Silly Billy!

Chloe Goult (10)
Carnagill CP School

The Street

Number 7 is a tall man with shiny eyes.
He wears posh shoes and a necklace
That dangles around his neck.
He is always comfortable.

Number 9 and 11 are identical twins,
They wear swanky shoes.
Both love their pipes which are always lit.
They have a huge driveway.

Number 13 is a giant, narrow man.
He has a brown shirt and swish trainers.
He can see his neighbours easily
Because he's so lofty.

Liam Auty (10)
Follifoot CE Primary School

The Street

Number seven is an independent man with sparkling eyes and a tall
stripy hat.
Peeping over at his next-door neighbours,
A dignified but bossy man,
Guarded by a line of straight soldiers.

Numbers nine and eleven are identical twin sisters,
Narrow, green, shiny eyes,
Small, skinny but elegant and wearing bright pink dresses,
Both have excellent fashion sense.

Number thirteen, a tall slim lady,
Colourfully dressed in her green skirt, with bright yellow eyeshadow,
A joyful, happy woman,
Looks after nature with care.

Millie Isaacson (9)
Follifoot CE Primary School

The Street

Number 7 is a smart young doctor with a nice-looking face.
With shiny blue eyes, looking down on his cool cars,
Thinking he's the best.

9 and 11, two young friends who always play together,
They have short, smart hair and huge feet,
Matching yellow eyes and big broad smiles,
With bright red trainers.

Number 13 is a lofty thin old man
Who's always very grumpy,
With a frown on his face, scowling at the world
With an unlucky badge in his chest.

William Caldecott (9)
Follifoot CE Primary School

The Street

Number 7 is a smart young MP,
He wears a big black hat and a black suit,
And big black shoes, looks smugly down on a Porsche 911,
Shiny eyes and black eyelashes,
And a chain of golden stars.

Number 9 and 11 are twins, who share the same eyes,
But 9 has black eyelashes and 11 has grey eyelashes,
Number 9 has a large footy cap,
But 11 doesn't have a hat.

Number 13 is a really unlucky lady, who would love to move out,
She would love to be 20 but not 60,
She has a dark brown necklace of dead flowers,
And she is tall and thin.

Ben Goddard (9)
Follifoot CE Primary School

The Street

Number 7 is a posh city man,
Wearing a black top hat and smart clothes,
And staring scornfully at the other houses.

11 and 9 are the best of friends,
One is smart and wise
And the other is cool and wicked.

13 is a tall thin man with a cigar in his mouth,
He's very hard on other people.

Number 15 is a short plump figure,
With an oversized coat,
Who wears a hat.

Daniel Walker (10)
Follifoot CE Primary School

The Street

The smart man at number 7 has a big afro
And gleaming, shiny shades
He watches down on his two Ferrari shoes
And he smokes a cigar.

9 and 11 are a pair of identical twins called Maria and Melissa
They have long bushy hair and pink and black beads
And they spend most of their time showing off
And arguing with each other.

The stylish lady at number 13
Is a bossy neighbour
She has bright shiny eyes and lilac eyeshadow
Her big black boots show off the scene.

Number 15 is a sad old lady,
She looks at the other houses on her street and hopes she will

be like them.

Her deep scars fill her face,
As she is pushed aside from the rest.

Number 17 is a chubby king
Who rules the street and his chuckles echo
His podgy tummy sticks out,
And his crown spikes through the air.

Isabelle Lee (9)
Follifoot CE Primary School

The Street

Number 7 is a tall, overweight gentleman,
He has a duvet to cover him,
He indulges in his lifestyle,
And looks down on his neighbours disdainfully.

Numbers 9 and 11 are a pair of greedy twins,
They look at number 7 and want all he has,
They have Aston Martins to rival number 7's Jaguars,
But they remain jealous.

Number 13 is a tall, slim lady,
With a very unlucky life,
Her red, sad eyes looking down on everyone but lonely,
She could never look back at a time when she was happy.

Number 15 is a tramp,
With grimy, unwashed skin ingrained with dirt,
His hair is a shaggy mess,
He needs no one to depend on.

Number 17 is a majestic city gentleman,
With well kept hair,
He looks at his neighbours with a wish to help them,
He has sparkling eyes and a mouth that never shuts up.

Benjamin Ball (9)
Follifoot CE Primary School

The Street

Number 7 is a posh city gentleman
He's looking down on the rest of the street.
Showing off his fast car,
As he puffs a cigarette.

Number 13 he is a lonely old man,
He is always sad.
He can never look back to a time he was happy,
The old man looks upon the street sadly.

Numbers 9 and 11 are a pair of silly twins,
They are always doing stuff wrong.
They can't please the rest of the street,
The silly twins are always annoying the old man at number 13.

Number 15 is a tramp
He is a lonely tramp
When he looks at the street nobody notices
He is looking for somebody to live there.

Number 17 is a funny man
He is always making jokes at number 7
And never cares about number 15
Nobody likes him at all.

Sophie Webster (9)
Follifoot CE Primary School

The Street

Number 7 is tall, thin lady,
She lights a cigarette and flashes her big wide eyes.
With long eyelashes,
And pointy shoes with white tights.

Number 9 and 11 are fat twins.
With long, thin hair and matching hats,
You can see a few wrinkles on their faces,
As they sit back and sprawl happily on their bright green carpet.

Number 13 is a slim lady with smart gleaming, glasses,
And a thin-lipped mouth,
She is very bossy and always gets her own way,
Her clothes are not dirty, in fact they are rather clean, with a smart
                                                    beaded necklace.

Number 15 is an old widow,
With drooping eyes and cracks in her face,
She frowns and her top hat is crushed
And covered in cobwebs.

Number 17 is a fat old man with cracked glasses,
A smart, grey suit and a matching tie,
He has sad eyes with a crushed, stripy hat,
No one to care for, no one to love because he's all by himself.

Charlotte Preston (9)
Follifoot CE Primary School

The Street

Number 7
Number 7 is a posh city gentleman,
Wearing a black top hat and smart clothes,
Standing importantly,
And frowning scornfully at his neighbours.

Numbers 9 and 11
Numbers 9 and 11 are two cheeky brothers,
They both have short dark hair and glasses
They are inseparable
And always cheerful.

Number 17
Number 17 is a old grandpa
His black walking stick by his side,
He has closed eyes that make him look very tired.
He has short, green straggly hair.

Laura Summersall (10)
Follifoot CE Primary School

The Street

Number 7 is a tall, stern lady,
A comfortable, smooth black hat perched on her head,
A piercing look in her eyes,
As she glares disdainfully at her unimportant neighbours.

Number 9 and 11 are close friends,
One snobbish and smart, one daring and adventurous,
But they both have fair, long hair and full, flowing skirts,
As they chat to others why are always pleasant.

Number 13 is a sturdy, hard man, with narrow eyes,
A crooked nose and a tight-lipped mouth,
A brave, proud look on his face,
He thinks he belongs elsewhere.

Milly Downing (10)
Follifoot CE Primary School

The Street

House number 7 is a fat, old man,
He looks down at his old friends,
He only thinks of himself now,
He is now always angry at his neighbours because he wants
everyone to be posh like him.

House number 9 is an old women,
Who wears a glass eye,
She wears a bright green T-shirt,
But she is a very kind women.

Number 13 is a towering, narrow women,
Who is a bully,
She wears a black T-shirt and trousers,
She is a mean woman.

House number 17 is a huge, lofty man,
He has lots of pet bats which fly around him,
No one has ever lived with him,
So he is lonely.

Harry Newis (10)
Follifoot CE Primary School

Cats

(Dedicated to my cat, Sparkle)

Cats are weird creatures
They're not at all like preachers
Cats are like cheetahs
And they're always climbing and playing
They're never ever staying
Cats are clever whatever the weather
They come in all different types
Tabby cats, black and white cats
Are cats weird creatures?

Ailsa Key (9)
Hambleton CE Primary School

The Frightened Bright Man

There once was a man who was incredibly bright
But the only thing he loved to do was sit and drink some Sprite
Then along came a ghost
Who fell into a post
And gave the man such a fright!

Gregor Anderson (10)
Hambleton CE Primary School

My Puppy

It's a white and brown dog
Who likes to jog.

Its got big blue eyes
And it likes to chase flies.

It hates rats
But lives to chase cats.

It always plays with squeaky toys
It makes plenty of noise.

It eats its dinner but it always wants more
It always acts like a bore!

Liam Turton (10)
Hambleton CE Primary School

Poems Everywhere

Poems here, poems there
Poems littering the air
I grab one, I read it
It makes me cry
I feel as if I'm going to die!

Gaby Dunwell (10)
Hambleton CE Primary School

Bellybopper

A dragon flies up in the sky,
How does he fly?
His mouth is a chopper,
He looks like a Bellybopper.

Can you see the wings so fast,
As he flies speedily past?
He's yellow, green, blue and red.
His mum puts him to sleep when he goes to bed.

Nicholas Redgrave (10)
Hambleton CE Primary School

Snaky Wakey

Some snakes play fake,
They slither and catch their prey.

Their tongues are like a pair of scissors,
They hiss all the time
And their bodies are warm.

Max Shaw (9)
Hambleton CE Primary School

Snaky

No, it is not a worm or a caterpillar,
Watch it slither, it could give you a shiver.
Its body is like a long, scaly tail,
Quite hard but looks so frail.
It catches its prey without fail.

James O'Farrell (10)
Hambleton CE Primary School

Spotty Otty Cheetah

(Dedicated to my cat, Ashton)

It's not a dragon or a snail,
it's a cheetah with a lovely tail.
It hunts around looking for mice,
or other things to slice.

When it's day it hunts for its prey,
and when it's night it sleeps away.
It pounces around all day long,
roaring a cheetah song.

Montana Baldwin (8)
Hambleton CE Primary School

Shaggy Dog

Shaggy Dog loves his log
But never likes the cat, Mog

When Dog spots him on his patch
He runs around, who can he catch?

He gobbles up his lunch
Like he can't stop, even if it's brunch.

Even though he eats like a dog
He does not run, he just jogs.

Charlotte Sackley (11)
Hambleton CE Primary School

A Knight, A Kite And A Fright

There once was a brave knight,
Who fell into a terrible fight,
He shot an arrow
But it hit a sparrow
And the sparrow flew into a kite in fright.

Lukanos Anderson (10)
Hambleton CE Primary School

Cheetah

He's faster than a gazelle and a hare
He's running about without a care.

His teeth are like knives
And he's got jet-black eyes.

He hunts in the night
When there is no light.

He goes up in his high tree, waiting for the next day
Ready to kill his prey.

Jamie Kilvington (10)
Hambleton CE Primary School

The Croc

Teeth as sharp as knives.
People stepped in and lost their lives.

Scales so rough.
As he is so tough.

Green as grass.
He swims past.

Sweeping through the water.
So silently and then . . .

Snap!

Liberty Hamilton (10)
Hambleton CE Primary School

The Wolf - Haiku

The wolf cries, it dies
The wind rustles through its fur
It makes the world stir.

Faith Muscroft (10)
Hambleton CE Primary School

My Dog

It's a beautiful chocolate milkshake dog.
Who likes to dig and find a log.

Its got gorgeous blue eyes.
And likes to chase flies.

It always plays with its squeaky toys.
It really makes plenty of noise.

Its got the softest, warmest, cleanest skin.
And it really hates the smell of a dirty bin.

It hates the taste of smelly old rats.
But loves to chase running cats.

It loves to play and have some fun.
But hates the sound of a shooting gun.

Its got a middle-sized tail.
And a doggie friend called Bail.

It loves to snuggle up warm and tight.
Right in front of the fire that's so light.

I love my dog, her name is Bailey.
We run and play together daily.

Louise Grice (10)
Hambleton CE Primary School

The Jaguar

The jaguar moves slowly through the grass
And the jaguar starts stalking the deer.
It gets closer and closer to its prey
It pounces onto its enemy.
It catches it and digs in
Finally it settles down in a tree
Ready for the next day.

Alex Heaton (9)
Hambleton CE Primary School

Dogs

Dogs can be all different colours such as black, ginger and white
Some dogs bite, some dogs don't
I prefer the dogs that don't bite
Dogs like to eat
Dogs walk in a beat
Dogs love to play
They also like to lead the way
They sleep cosy
But they are very noisy
Dogs can be small or tall
But sometimes they climb up walls
They sit in boots
They are very, very cute!

Jo-Anne Stirzaker (10)
Hambleton CE Primary School

Vroom!

Vroom!
The car goes by
Neon lights flashing bright
Sound of the speaker blaring loud
The exhaust roaring one-hundred miles per hour down the street
He can hear a police car in the distance
The police shoot the wheel
He jumps out of the car
He's gone too far
Landing on the nails
This careless driver is now off to jail.

Harley Copley (10)
Hambleton CE Primary School

Loudly

Loudly the kitchen pans go *smash!*
Loudly a woman hears the drums go *bash!*
Loudly a girl turns the music up.
Loudly a man drops the china cups.

Loudly the man bashes the pan.
Loudly the woman smashes the cups.
Loud the shouts, but loudest of all
A woman screaming at the man at the door.

Antonia Nolan (9)
Hambleton CE Primary School

Slowly

Slowly the flower blooms
Slowly the hooves of a horse walk
Slowly my dog goes dancing

Slowly my best friend comes and watches
But, slowest of all, I walk home on the old brick wall.

Emily Fox (8)
Hambleton CE Primary School

Loudly

Loudly the chainsaw cuts the wood
Loudly the crowd cheers at the football match
Loudly the tiger growls at the elephants
Loudly the telephone rings in the library
Loudly the bird squawks at the lion
Loudly the monkey screams at the bird
Loudly the engine goes on the car
Loud the bull charges into the boy
The boy is crying.

Oliver Twidale (9)
Hambleton CE Primary School

Loudly

Loudly the chainsaw cuts the wood
Loudly the crowd cheers at the football match
Loudly the tiger growls at the elephants
Loudly the telephone rings in the library
Loudly the person sings a song
Loudly the aeroplane engine goes on
Loudly the dog barks at the man . . .
Loud the lightning but loudest of all is the baby crying.

Scott Arnold (9)
Hambleton CE Primary School

Happily

Happily the ducks swim in the pond
Happily the puppies play with a ball
Happily the puffin dives to catch fish
Happily the bird loops in the sky

Happily the owner clips on the rosette
Happily the bunny munches his carrot
Happy the animals, but happiest of all . . .
The horses gallop around the field.

Emily Wilson (9)
Hambleton CE Primary School

Inside

Inside a plant pot is a jungle,
Inside a football is a winning goal.
Inside an acorn a tree waits,
Inside a shell there's an open ocean,
Inside a dandelion seed is a clock,
Inside an egg a chicken farm,
Inside a book is a tale to tell.

Abigail Haley (8)
Hambleton CE Primary School

Loudly

Loudly the dog barked at my house (woof!)
Loudly the porcupine screeched when I was at the safari park (eeek!)
Loudly the bird tweeted in its nest (tweet!)
Loudly the tiger roared in its cage (roar!)
Loudly the cat miaowed at my dad (miaow!)
Loudly the drill drilled in my garden (drill!)
Loudly the cow mooed on the farm (mooooo!)
Loudly the school played in the playground
But loudest of all is my dad screaming at me in the hall.

Alex Bernard (8)
Hambleton CE Primary School

Slowly

Slowly I creep along the street.
Slowly my tummy wants to eat.
Slowly the polar bears climb on icebergs.
Slowly children watch a flying bird.

Slowly the ice cream drips down my hand.
Slowly I hear a band.
Slowly I hear a faint ring of a bell.
Slowly the tortoise tries to get out of its shell.

Charlotte Tate (8)
Hambleton CE Primary School

Computer

Computers are clever,
Computers are smart,
Everyone must like computers.
They have the internet and games and other things too.
You can print and copy and buy things to go with it as well.
Oh, computers are swell!

Richard Jones (9)
Hambleton CE Primary School

Loudly

Loudly I scream at the man at the door
Loudly I stamp on the floor
Loudly the dogs in garden bark
Loudly the car gets ready to park

Loudly the cars honk their horns
Loudly the mower mows the lawns
Loudly the engine roars - but loudest of all
The lion roars over the old brick wall.

Rachel Rhiannon Hollingworth (8)
Hambleton CE Primary School

Loudly

Loudly the chainsaw cuts the wood
Loudly the crowd cheers at the football match
Loudly the tiger growls at the elephants
Loudly the telephone rings in the library
Loudly the elephant toots
Loudly the dog barks
Loudly the lightning comes down
Loud the baby cries but . . .
Loudest of all, a punk rocker sings!

Luke Pendlebury (8)
Hambleton CE Primary School

Loudly

Loudly the chainsaw cuts the wood.
Loudly the crowd cheers at the football match.
Loudly the tiger growls at the elephants.
Loudly the telephone rings in the library.
Loudly the karaoke machine sings.
Loudly the lightning struck.
Loudly the dog barked his head off.
Loudly the aeroplane flew past me.

Paul Campbell (9)
Hambleton CE Primary School

Turtle Soup

He's not a snail or a worm
He's a turtle and his name is Lurm

His shell is like a rock
Sometimes he will give people a shock

He scares the kids to death
And even the head chef

He has stubby legs
And he loves to eat eggs

One day the chef cuts him with a knife
And that was the end of his life.

Thomas Kneen (10)
Hambleton CE Primary School

Girhyme

(Dedicated to my mum)

Giraffes have spots
And like to eat from treetops
They have big lips to help them eat
For them, it's a long way to their feet.

They have long necks, obviously
So they can see over the tallest tree
They walk with their heads up high
Their heads head up into the sky.

Olivia Mitchell (9)
Hambleton CE Primary School

Slowly

Slowly the tide drowns the sand.
Slowly the mist crosses the land.
Slowly the child heaves up the old grey horse and rides a mile.
Slowly the old woman walks the stile.

Slowly the hands of the ruined clock go tick-tock.
Slowly the damp dew dries on the dock.
Slowly goes the crooked snail.
But slowest of all . . .
The old moss on the knocked-down wall.

Billy Giorgia Ratcliffe (8)
Hambleton CE Primary School

A Pocket Of Rhyme

A pocket of rhyme,
Worth more than a dime.
This book is bursting at the seams,
With poems and dreams.
Don't spoil your head,
Or go to bed.
Take a look,
Inside this book.
Imagine the wind whispering in the trees,
Listen to the words of the bees.

Alex Davies (10)
Hambleton CE Primary School

Loudly

Loudly the woman screams at the man
Loudly the lion roars at the mouse
Loudly the dolphin splashes the tourists
Loudly the birds go *cheep cheep!*

Loudly the school bell rings and screams everywhere
Loudly the rain crashes in the window
Loudly an owl goes *tu-whit tu-whoo* - but loudest of all,
It's my brother running into the wall!

Leah Charlotte Roberts (8)
Hambleton CE Primary School

Loudly

Loudly the camel coughs at my dad's face
Loudly a pelican stands in the sea
Loudly my dog barks at a visitor
Loudly the road works drill annoyingly
Loudly the crowd cheers
Loudly the wave's splash high
Loudly my brother's fallout
Loudly the geese fly over my house
Loudly the children play in the playground
But loudest of all is my brother screaming in the hall.

Matthew James Gelder (8)
Hambleton CE Primary School

Football

I once was playing football
When I was trying to hit the wall with the ball
I hit the bully in the face
I ran but he could keep up with my pace
In the end it turned into a big brawl.

Jordan Leybourn (10)
Hambleton CE Primary School

I Wish I Was A Cat

Sleek and black,
Running round the garden
In pitch-black night.
Hiding in shadows,
Not to be seen,
Catching mice.
Hissing at dogs,
Jumping up trees.
Keeping a lookout,
And running away,
Back to a snug, cosy basket!

Ellie Hore (8)
Osmotherley CP School

The Black Cat

A shadow on the street,
Sniffing in the dustbins,
Thinking what it will eat.
A jet-black shadow,
Roaming about the street.
Purring, miaowing.
Greeny-yellow eyes
That you can always see.

Sam Liburd (8)
Osmotherley CP School

My Pony

R oyal is his name.
O ats are his favourite.
Y ou'd love him like he was yours.
A little Red Rum galloping full flat!
L aughing boy is his nickname.

Sally Hughlock (10)
Osmotherley CP School

The Lion

I hunt my prey
Day and night,
Never stopping for breath,
I keep running,
I keep running.

I eat my prey
Day and night,
Food is delicious,
I keep eating,
I keep eating.

I stalk my prey
Day and night,
Watching carefully,
I keep stalking,
I keep stalking.

I am the pride
Of all the animals,
Being proud is good,
I am proud,
I am proud.

Proud to be the king!

Liam Turner (10)
Osmotherley CP School

My Dog, Finn

My dog, Finn, eats strawberry laces,
My dog, Finn, eats roast lamb.
My dog, Finn, runs away to explore,
My dog, Finn, chases a ball in the field.
My dog, Finn, chased sheep,
My dog, Finn, swims in the sea!

My dog, Finn.

Nick Foxton (10)
Osmotherley CP School

Animals Of Our World

The soft whisper of the crickets,
The loud roar of the leopard,
The king of the jungle claiming his prey,
In a distant barn the barn owl is watching the hay.

The slither of the snake,
The *baa* of a sheep,
The giraffe rising with its high neck,
Minnows darting through their beck.

The shark eyeing its prey,
The chicken laying the farmer's dinner,
The mice eating their cheese not knowing it is a trap,
The eagle hunting his prey, not stopping for a nap.

We must all look after these animals,
They also share the world,
We must learn to care,
From the minute newt to the ferocious bear.

James Marriott (11)
Osmotherley CP School

My Dog, Jip

My dog, Jip,
Loves to run around,
He rounds up the sheep,
Hunts out the rabbits.

He stretches a bit,
Pounces a lot,
He barks at people,
O, I love my dog, Jip.

Nathan Adam Wood (7)
Osmotherley CP School

If I Were A Cheetah

If I were a cheetah I would hunt all night.
If I were a cheetah I would run as fast as the speed of light.
If I were a cheetah I would sleep in the tops of the trees.
If I were a cheetah I would pull my prey up on the trees where others
                                                couldn't reach.

I start at my prey . . .
Suddenly I hear a distant *bang! Bang!*
It gets louder and louder.
My eyes light up with
Fear and fright.

Esther Torniley-Walker (10)
Osmotherley CP School

My Cat, Whiskey

My cat, Whiskey, is brown and gold,
She eats cat meat,
And does what she's told,
She likes to sit next to the fire by my feet.

She watches the fish bowl,
She likes a cuddle,
She once caught a mole,
And she never gets in trouble for making a puddle.

She's twelve years old,
She's scared of a ball,
She likes her hold,
And she's very small.

Joseph Wood (10)
Osmotherley CP School

My Dog, Herbie

My dog, Herbie,
Is the newest dog yet,
A black Labrador,
As black as jet,
He races with me,
Like he doesn't care,
We go racing everywhere.

My dog, Herbie,
Licks his paw,
Just as if he rules the world,
He acts as though he's the law,
He eats his food
And loves it so,
He looks as if he has been glued to the bowl.
My dog, Herbie.

Harry Brass (10)
Osmotherley CP School

Egypt

Hot,
Dusty hotels,
Swimming pools,
Busy, busy.
Big country,
Lots of cars.
Lots of people,
Taxis, taxis.
Camels and deserts.
Hot, hot,
Hot.

William Marriott (7)
Osmotherley CP School

Animals Of The Farm

Animals of the farm,
Ducks, geese and turkeys,
Ready for Christmas,
Tasty and juicy for the winter.

Animals of the farm,
Chicks, lambs and kittens,
All born in spring
Cuddling but meaning no harm.

Animals of the farm,
Flies flying and annoying the animals,
This all happens in summer,
Flies are buzzing but they mean no harm.

Animals of the farm,
All coming in for winter,
They don't care,
Because they're escaping the cold winter air.

Joe Allison (10)
Osmotherley CP School

If I Was A Cow

If I was a cow . . .

I would moo all day.
My friends would say
I was insane.
I would moo at a plane.

If I got stuck up a tree
My friends would flee
When the branch went *snap!*
I would hit the ground with a *slap!*

William Stamp (10)
Osmotherley CP School

I Like Noises

I like the kettle tooting,
I like the owl hooting,
I like the hoover whirring,
And also the cat purring.

I like the tap dripping,
And the horn of the car pipping,
I like the dog woofing,
I like the sound of my dad puffing.

I like the snap,
With the tap,
I like the sound of the pan,
Banging on the man.

But, most of all,
I like the sound of me,
Buzzing in the tree,

Megan Eustace (10)
St Mary's Primary School, Knaresborough

Day At The Beach!

It is a lovely sunny day here at Rydell,
But people are not having fun,
Doing homework, sleeping and all things boring.

I say to myself, how boring are they?
So I sing . . . you should be having fun
Get playing in the sea, no time for
Sleeping, come on, let's have a blast!
Party, party, party, party!
Come on, have fun at Rydell!

Nicola Milligan (9)
St Mary's Primary School, Knaresborough

Deep In The Forest

In the forest there are witches, wizards and ghouls
Most of them are really big fools,
Never walk into the forest alone, you never know just
                                    what might happen,
Because there are witches and ghouls
The real big fools
So never walk into the forest.

One night there was a party of ten,
Carrying a real big hen.
So the witches and wizards got out their wands,
And zapped the party of ten!
Everyone but the hen,
So there's the story,
In all its glory,
So *never* go into the forest!

Patrick Sunley (9)
St Mary's Primary School, Knaresborough

The Opposite World

Yes means no and no means yes
Hi means goodbye, goodbye means hi
Left is right and right is left
Up is down, down is up
Winter is autumn and spring is summer
Autumn is winter, summer is spring.

A tornado is a twirl of good weather
And good weather is a tornado
'Jordan, Jordan, time for school'
'Already? It's only been 5 minutes!'

Jordan Firth (9)
St Mary's Primary School, Knaresborough

Planes

Harrier jump jets and Tornados,
Spitfires and Hurricanes,
Rolls-Royce engines and weapons,
All come on planes.

747s and 777s,
Concorde and Mach 2,
Go well with passengers,

While Halifax, Lancaster,
B52 and Junker 88s
Are bombers.

But, to me, planes are planes,
No matter what you call them,
They are all the same,
Planes, planes, planes.

Thomas Brennan (9)
St Mary's Primary School, Knaresborough

The Dragon

There's a dragon,
In a castle,
With big sharp teeth and
Spiky claws,
Its tail is covered in spikes,
It breathes scorching flames of fire,
Waiting for a knight to save the princess,
Every time a knight tries he ends up black and on the wall,
So the next time a knight comes, don't run into the dragon
Otherwise you will end up black and on the wall.

Jacob Fincham Dukes (9)
St Mary's Primary School, Knaresborough

Dance

I like to dance, I like to sing
All my dancers have a bit of bling
I get a wonderful feeling inside
It makes me feel I want to glide!

Whizzing here, whizzing there
I never seem to really care
If my dance and song are any good
I don't feel I really should

I really want to become a star
Listen, la-di la-di dah
Modern, tap and ballet
I did a dance in the school play

A rhythm always will come soon
I dance all night until the moon
Comes out and shines right on my feet
Then I find a beat.

Eleanor Churchill (9)
St Mary's Primary School, Knaresborough

About My Dog

My dog is cool
He likes walks and chasing cats and climbing trees
He is really quite peculiar
He is as fast as lightning
When you run in front of him you get knocked over by him
It is very funny!

Louie Barker (9)
St Mary's Primary School, Knaresborough

Stinky Trolls

Stinky trolls smell triple the smell we do,
I was flabbergasted when one stood on me,
Its eyes were like dinner plates,
Although the troll's huge, its brain was the size of a flea!

Trolls eat human flesh,
So you'd better be careful,
I saw one in a zoo before, surrounded by mesh,
Once it felt very tearful, so it burst into tears!

Adena Keeys (9)
St Mary's Primary School, Knaresborough

Lions!

Lions are lovely,
Wild things and free,
As fast as the wind is,
As strong as the sea.

Lions are lovely,
Smoother than silk.

Lions are lovely,
Gentle as milk.

Lions are lovely,
They roar like a storm.

Lions are lovely,
They're soft and they're warm!

Libby Owens (10)
St Mary's Primary School, Knaresborough

Peace In My World . . .

Peace is a healthy, soothing fruit salad.
With a side order of melted chocolate and fudge cake!
Peace is a tropical island with some breeze in the air,
There are lovely fruits everywhere, oh, look over there, ooh; pear.
Peace is a sweetie-pie singing lots of songs,
Eating a chicken pie that tastes *yum-yum!*
So keep peace rolling in!

Rachel Jackson (9)
St Mary's RC Primary School, Selby

Peace

Peace is stillness everywhere
Like a gentle breeze in the air
When the wind blows, the palm trees sway
That will be a happy day.

Peace is gentleness everywhere
When clouds are floating in the air
In the high sky birds fly by
Giving a little tweet, saying hi.

Ruby Waterworth (9)
St Mary's RC Primary School, Selby

Peace

Peace begins with telling God your sins,
Peace begins with staying calm,
Peace begins with staying praying to God,
Peace begins with making friends,
Peace begins with loving your family.

Beth Keeble (9)
St Mary's RC Primary School, Selby

Don't Take Lives, Take Love

Lying in a bed of poppies,
I thought about the day ahead.
A peaceful garden full of trees,
Then a thought popped into my head.
How are these wars going to stop
When they are attacking each other?
All they need is love to stick them back together.

Shannon Nee (10)
St Mary's RC Primary School, Selby

Take Love Not Lives

Once stood a beautiful valley
Now it's drawn to battle
With the guns giving a rattle
The tanks roaring and men shouting
Suddenly it stops . . .
happy world is born
A killing world dies
Take love not lives.

Chloe Grundy (11)
St Mary's RC Primary School, Selby

Peace

Peace is a picture
that you see when
you close your
eyes - everyone
being kind and
loving to each other.

Amy Grundy (10)
St Mary's RC Primary School, Selby

Sway With The Wind!

Lush green leaves sway with the wind
The image is tender, calm and quiet
Blue sky is light when the sun is shining
Evening comes into action
A beautiful sunset arrives
The sea is peaceful far, far away
Poppies rock in harmony
The world is quiet and tranquil
It feels happy!

Hannah Savage (10)
St Mary's RC Primary School, Selby

Peace

Flowers grow now war is over
Peace is now restored
Weapons are gone and the sun shines on
Peace is now restored
People are glad now war is over
Peace is now restored.

Hayley Dalrymple (10)
St Mary's RC Primary School, Selby

Peace Is Wonderful

Peace is wonderful
Peace is calm
Peace is quiet
Peace is lovely
Peace is the best thing in the world.

Jamie Graley (9)
St Mary's RC Primary School, Selby

Peace

Peace is like water dripping from your hand
Peace is like walking in the forest
Peace is like picking flowers

Peace is like snow in the winter
Peace is like a cloud in the sky
Peace is like dreaming in your sleep

Peace is like walking in the snow
Peace is like sitting in the sun
Peace is like walking across a field

Peace is like painting a rainbow
Peace is like reading a book
Peace is like catching butterflies.

Niall Sullivan & Malachi Brown (8)
St Mary's RC Primary School, Selby

Peace

Peace is like waves washing upon the sand,
Peace is like when your friend takes your hand,
Peace is like us side by side,
Peace is like when our sins have died.

Peace is like a heart full of love,
Peace is like a flying dove,
Peace is like a sunny summer's day,
Peace is when we start to pray.

Philippa Clay (8)
St Mary's RC Primary School, Selby

Peace

Peace is a rainbow after a storm
Peace is a quiet time to be alone.

Nicole Hey (8)
St Mary's RC Primary School, Selby

Peace

Peace is a feather
Falling from the sky
It is silence
In wintertime.

Peace is silence
When you pray
Peace is an ice cube
Melting in the sun.

Peace is a raindrop
Falling from the
Blue sky.

Peace is a rainbow
After a storm
Peace is a leaf dropping
From a tree.

Gabrielle Cooke (8)
St Mary's RC Primary School, Selby

Peace

Peace is like the thing called love,
Peace is like a flying dove
Looking over the cliff's edge
At the scene of peace
Peace comes when
The world sleeps.

Sean Corrigan (8)
St Mary's RC Primary School, Selby

The Peace In My Head

Peace is a lamb walking across a field
Walking though flowers that have colourful petals
Doves in the sky with beautiful white snowy wings
And a whole family of them flying away gracefully.

Peace is a breeze as you stand at your door
Watching your dog playing about with a ball
Happy as I am standing here at my door
You can smell a dinner been made for you

Peace is a book that you're reading in the sun
Butterfly flies on your book as you're reading it
You see its wings so colourful and bright
And then it flies away to a bush where some other butterflies are.

Kellie Nee (9)
St Mary's RC Primary School, Selby

Peace

Peace is like a cloud
In the sky
Peace is like a walk
In the snow
Peace is like sitting
In the sun
Peace is like reading
In your room
Peace is like sleeping
In your bed.

Niall Coulthard (8)
St Mary's RC Primary School, Selby

Peace

Peace begins when you make a friend
Peace begins when you listen to music
Peace begins when you pray
Peace begins when you lay in bed and daydream.

Alex Keeble (9)
St Mary's RC Primary School, Selby

The Daydream Dragon

The daydream dragon
Whips my mind away
To a sparkling land of my own . . .

His eyes are deep blue
Like the sky on a summer's evening
His friendly gaze so tempting.

His scales are smooth and patterned
The colour of crystals.

His teeth are small and white
Gleaming and unfrightening.

His claws are small and curved
Jewelled with snowy diamonds
Holding a gentle but firm grip around my mind.

His select and small size
Does not affect
The power he holds
In the classroom.

There is a daydream dragon
Inside of me
Who whips my mind away
To a sparkling land of my own . . .

Katie Bruce (11)
Spofforth CE Primary School

The Magic Box

(Based on 'Magic Box' by Kit Wright)

I will put in my box . . .

A Sylvania song smothered in chocolate
A gigantic penguin plodding through the scorching desert
The second brick of the Eiffel Tower struggling to get free.

I will put in my box . . .

A dynamic doll waiting to be played with
The first step of a baby girl and the last song of a grandpa
A silent snake with six feet.

My box is fashioned from silver and gold
With circles and squares on the lid
And smiles on the corners
Its hinges are the claws of birds.

I shall parachute in my box
From the top of Mount Everest
Then fall onto the flowery, green grass.

Katie Booth (9)
Spofforth CE Primary School

The Mix-Up Dragon

Nograd's nostrils cook my special sausages every Saturday.
My dragon sheds it skin every five minutes for silky carpets
                                                and curtains.
Inside of me there is a pleading dragon desperate to get
                                        her allowance.
Her silky scales are a burning red, handy for the cold winter nights.
When she's got a cold it's a disaster, there's a fire brigade out every
                                        time she sneezes.
Inside of me is a playful dragon, with four sisters and one brother.
My dragon will always be the same and she will always keep
to the rules and whisk me away to a land of my own.

Charlotte Freeman (10)
Spofforth CE Primary School

The Magic Box

(Based on 'Magic Box' by Kit Wright)

I will put in my box . . .

Penguins flying over the scorching ice of Antartica.
Lively bones, getting ready for the disco.
A distant memory from a Greek god.

I will put in my box . . .

A golden article written by the silver-winged gryphons.
A spiky slug emerging
from the wet marshy grass of the Sahara Desert.
A slimy snake that has flown from the icy plains of Antartica.

I will put in my box . . .

A beating heart from Tutankhamun.
A Viking boat that's sailing the seven seas.
A silent speech from a howling werewolf.

My box is fashioned from . . .
Snakeskin, with diamonds at its hinges.
The corners are bits of platinum,
With mysteries in the corner and
Devils on the lid.

I will skate in my box,
Past the sun and stars,
Smash into a rocket,
That takes me back to Mars.

Christopher Horne (10)
Spofforth CE Primary School

The Magic Box

(Based on 'Magic Box' by Kit Wright)

I shall put in my box . . .

The boiling dunes of the freezing cold Sahara
The last shot of an ancient air rifle
The mystical song of an ancient Greek siren

I shall put in my box . . .

A six-foot chicken slaughtering a helpless human
The deadly silence of St James' Park after a home win
Greeting cards sent by a Maori tribe

I shall put in my box . . .

The distant howl of a prowling werewolf
The look of glee on a child's face as he opens his birthday presents
The helpless cry of a slave

My box is fashioned from snakeskin and gas
With gems on the lid and wishes in the corners
I shall fly in my box over the golden coast of Australia
Then glide into space and far, *far away!*

Nicholas Honey (10)
Spofforth CE Primary School

Dexter The Dragon

Dexter's head is bigger than a plane.
His eyes are like glinting diamonds.
His claws are like a butcher's knife.
His scales are harder than gold.
His nostrils are like a chimney.
His breath smells like garlic.
His fire blast can knock eighteen blocks of flats down.

Joe Horne (9)
Spofforth CE Primary School

The Magic Box

(Based on 'Magic Box' by Kit Wright)

I will put in my box . . .

The silent tick from a clock going back in time
A song from the sun on an icy day
A tiny mountain from the USA

I will put in my box . . .

The first word from a giant baby
A cow from the freezing cold desert
The last scream from a pencil case

My box is fashioned from gold
With silver on top of the lid
The hinges are made from lightsabres

I will drive a boat in my box
And wash ashore on a sandy beach
The colour of the sun

Samuel Goddard (10)
Spofforth CE Primary School

The Dragon Poem

The teacher dragon eats you
If you don't listen
The bird dragon watches you
Like a hawk

The book dragon tears your books
When you're not looking
The homework dragon eats your homework
At night

The mountain dragon makes earthquakes
With his roar
The sea dragon makes a tidal wave
With his tail.

Thomas Goldring (10)
Spofforth CE Primary School

The Dragon Poem

The tail of the dragon is made of a rune flail with a ball.
The spine of the dragon is like the tip of a blade.
The eyes of a dragon are like two suns that can make you
blind immediately.
The ears are steel and can hear from 20km away.

Inside of me is a typing dragon that can type a sentence
in three seconds.
Inside of me is an engineering dragon that can make a cannonball
within a flash.
Inside of me is a smelting dragon that can make anything
with a hand.

The thinking dragon can answer any question you ask him to.
The air dragon can put air all over our solar system.
The disguised dragon can turn you into anything you want.
The life dragon can raise people from the dead.

Damon Hammond (9)
Spofforth CE Primary School

Up In The Attic

When up in the attic you go to explore
These are the things you'll find on the floor
My mum's old dolls' clothes
A white Christmas tree
Mum's smelly old hose
And old, ruined football
My own rotten jam
Broken, snapped crayons
My own rusty pram
A dusty suitcase
Mum's broken dolls' house
My own old, dead mouse
A rusty TV

What's up in the attic?

Tobias Mitchell (9)
Woodthorpe Primary School

What's Up In The Attic?

When up attic steps you go to explore
You'll find on the floor
These are the things
A pretend rose
A bag of baubles
Ancient baby clothes
A boxed Christmas tree
A big rusty base
Some blue ballet things
An orange suitcase
Sacks of dusty bears
And lots of old boats
A demolished tent
Some decaying coats
Dull Hallowe'en things

What's up in the attic?

Chloe Fletcher (9)
Woodthorpe Primary School

Autumn

The leaves falling
And changing colour
The wind zooming in the sky
Squirrels collecting acorns
Ready to eat
Conkers falling on the ground
The rain splashing on the path
Children jump in the leaves
The bare branches falling to the ground
The animals getting ready to hibernate
Horses in the stables sleeping
The squirrels getting food for their families
Badgers getting food
And running home to sleep to hibernate
The birds swooping in the sky.

Erin Morgan (7)
Woodthorpe Primary School

What's Up In The Attic?

You go to explore
    When up in the attic
        You'll find on the floor . . .
            These are the things
                A smashed jar of jam
                    With a broken wheel
                        An old, damp pram
                            A non-working train
                                A big box of fun
                                    Some vicious rats
                                        An old pellet gun
                                            Some dirty boys' toys
                                                With no shoe laces
                                                    Some old 90's shoes
                                                        And some suitcases
                                                            A big aeroplane

What's up in the attic?

Tony Fowler (10)
Woodthorpe Primary School

Autumn

Flowing leaves passing by.
Powerful winds blasting by you.
Spinning leaves, flying like an aeroplane.
Children finding brown, green and red leaves.

Nuts being found by little, quiet squirrels.
Hedgehogs, rabbits and other animals hibernate.
Autumn leaves,
Twisting, twirling and talking.

It's autumn, hooray!

Cameron Loftus (7)
Woodthorpe Primary School

What's Up In The Attic?

Up in the attic
You'll go to explore
When up attic stairs
You'll find on the floor
These are the things
Some old rusty hooks
A dog called Tim
Some new Christmas books
An old teddy bear
Some broken old lights
12 coloured pencils
Some dusty old tights
And one cuckoo clock
An old gargoyle called me
Lays on the floor
Some old marbles
A snapped Christmas tree

What's up in the attic?

Amy Martyn (10)
Woodthorpe Primary School

In My Fridge

In my fridge there's nothing much
But come over here and have a touch.

10 carrots
9 grapes
8 yoghurts in all sizes and shapes
7 strawberries
6 chocolate bars
5 tomatoes
Oh yes, lots of jars
4 sprouts
3 Chocolate Shreddies
2 milks
1 chocolate teddy, *tasty!*

Natasha Askew (9)
Woodthorpe Primary School

What's Up In The Attic?

You go to explore
   When up in the attic
      You'll find on the floor
         These are the things
            A toy wishing well
               And some ancient clothes
                  An old Christmas bell
                     Some popped footballs
                        And a filthy tree
                           A tatty old suitcase
                           A picture of me
                           A busted freezer
                              Some old, rusty trains
                                 There are some big boxes
                                 And a big train
                                   An odd looking toy!

Thomas Murden (9)
Woodthorpe Primary School

Autumn

Is the time when leaves are falling,
Some are soft, spiralling rough leaves,
Swirling in the breeze,
Leaves curling round and round.

I like it when the leaves turn
   red,
   yellow,
   brown and
   green.

Jordan Bryszkiewski (7)
Woodthorpe Primary School

What's Up In The Attic?

You go to explore
    When up attic steps
        You'll find on the floor
            These are the things
                Some interesting rocks
                    Fifty fiddle bows
                        Two damp kitchen clocks
                        An empty suitcase
                        The skin of a bat
                        Old raffle tickets
                          A filthy dead rat
                          A shattered TV
                            Some big fishing hooks
                            A Christmas treetop
                              Dusty old joke books
                              Some empty boxes

What's up in the attic?

Alex Frasina (9)
Woodthorpe Primary School

Autumn

Autumn fills the ground with leaves.
Autumn makes the floor colourful
With loads of leaves and petals.
I'm amazed when the leaves fall off the trees.

Autumn's the best time of your life.
Autumn is near Christmas.
Autumn is still a little bit warm,
But sometimes it can be cold.

Chloe Robertson (8)
Woodthorpe Primary School

Up In The Attic

You go to explore
When up attic steps
You'll find on the floor
These are the things
A grey special tool
A Hornby train set
A long swimming pool
A yellow plant pot
A box of red stars
A destroyed red train
Some pictures from Mars
Some old children's toys
An old box of cars
A creamy trifle
Some old paperwork
A pellet rifle

What's up in the attic?

Robert Smith (9)
Woodthorpe Primary School

Winter

Winter is coming
It's creeping down my street.
Grabbing my wellies,
Putting them on my feet.

Make a family,
From a blanket of snow.
I can smell roast dinner,
I think my dad's burnt the chicken though.

Natasha Healey (9)
Woodthorpe Primary School

What's Up In The Attic?

You go to explore
When up attic steps
You'll find on the floor
These are the things
Lots of dull boats
And a demolished tent
Some ruined old coats
A boxed Christmas tree
And a pretend rose
Some safety gates
And some baby clothes
Some tatty old doors
And a teddy bear
A dusty old tree
Some scratty old hair

What's up in the attic?

Amy Rowlinson (10)
Woodthorpe Primary School

Autumn

Wind, wind
Conkers dropping down
Leaves crackling
Brown, dying plants
Trees sad and scary
Rain tippling down on you
Animals trying to hibernate.

Ella Duke (7)
Woodthorpe Primary School

What's Up In The Attic?

When up attic steps you go to explore
    You'll find on the floor
        These are the things
            A broken RV
                Holes in huge clothes
                    A smashed black TV
                      Broken-up games
                          Wet, damp, ripped-up hats
                        A rusty old rock
                          A box of cute cats
                          A dusty skeleton
                            Some gigantic buns
                              Silly, weird boys' games
                            A set of old guns
                              A shattered window

What's up in the attic?

Jack Allinson (9)
Woodthorpe Primary School

Autumn

Colourful flowers grow up high in the sky, blowing gently.
Leaves spinning and green, shiny leaves blowing
Round and round, like little helicopters.
Wind is whooshing round and round and round.
The sun shining out brightly
Kids are playing happily in the sun,
The sky is bright blue.

Megan Brittain (8)
Woodthorpe Primary School

What's Up In The Attic?

A broken square clock
A ghost and
A box of felt tips
A huge petrol tank
A rat that was fighting
And old wobbly bottles
Old tarantula food
An old dead rat
An old baby pram
And a pair of socks
A toy that said damn!
Some very old clocks
I saw a pram
And an old toy box
Shoes that are Nike
Two jars of red jam
An old rusty bike

What's up in the attic?

Declan Barnett (9)
Woodthorpe Primary School

A Poem About Autumn

Flowing leaves passing,
Blustery wind making
Leaves spin off trees.

Leaves scatter along the grass,
Spiky leaves falling from the trees.

Smooth red, yellow, brown leaves,
Falling from the trees.

Chloe Muggeridge (7)
Woodthorpe Primary School

What's Up In The Attic?

You go to explore
  When up attic steps
    You'll find on the floor
      These are the things
        Trousers with a tear
          Old raffle tickets
            A dusty blue bear
              Dad's ancient red ties
                Poison to kill bats
                  An old kitchen bowl
                    A box of old mats
                      Remains of our tent
                        Long, red, smelly socks
                          A dead, filthy cat
                            A broken square box
                              Two jars of red blood

What's up in the attic?

Thomas Pannet (9)
Woodthorpe Primary School

Autumn

Leaves are falling off the trees in autumn.
Leaves change colour to red, yellow and even orange.
The trees go bald when the leaves fall off in autumn.
Leaves are falling off the trees in autumn.
The leaves change colour to red, yellow and even orange.
Autumn wind sometimes can be rough
And sometimes can be smooth.

Daniel Corr (7)
Woodthorpe Primary School

What's Up In the Attic?

You go to explore
When up attic steps
You'll find on the floor
These are the things
Some dictionaries
A little black cat
A glittering tree
A smelly green mat
A spider, a cockroach
My Mum's and Dad's whips
My teddy dog, Dan
A set of blue ships
A picture of me
A toy wishing well
A roaring lion cub
A box of old spells

What's up in the attic?

Michelle Dupley (9)
Woodthorpe Primary School

Autumn

Autumn is my favourite time of year.
Squirrels make their nests,
Squirrels gather their nuts.
The wind is very strong and swirly.
The leaves rush round and round.
I love jumping in the piles of leaves!

Naomi Martyn (7)
Woodthorpe Primary School

Up In The Attic

You go to explore
    When up attic steps
        You will find the floor
            These are the things
                A rubbish dolls' house
                    A tatty suitcase
                        An outdated mouse
                            Little baby clothes
                                And some dated rats
                                  My dad's little toys
                                    Seven smelly bats
                                        An out of date tree
                                          Some old rotten jam
                                      A broken TV
                                            A old, collapsed pram
                                            Old, frayed boxes

What's up in the attic?
Kayley Bayston (9)
Woodthorpe Primary School

Yellow

Yellow is the sun, rising for another day,
Yellow is daffodils, swaying in the wind,
Yellow is the sand, beside the big blue sea,
Yellow is the stars, twinkling in the night sky,
Yellow is my ice cream, melting in the sun,
Yellow is a banana, which monkeys love to eat,
Yellow is the lightning strike from the sky,
Yellow is my favourite colour!

Shumi Miah (11)
Woodthorpe Primary School

Autumn

In autumn, on the trees, the leaves dance off.
Gold and brown, yellow and green,
Any colours you can see,
And in the dark the lightning goes *crash!*

Why do the leaves roughly fall off the trees?
Why does the lightning go *crash, bang, crash*?

When you step out of that door,
It will be freezing, dark and cold,
While you are wanting to be at home
And when you get in, a hot chocolate,
Nice and cosy laying in bed,
And after that you will fall fast asleep.

Zach Dodson (8)
Woodthorpe Primary School

Up in The Attic

You go to explore
When up attic steps
You'll find on the floor
These are the things
Old cricket wickets
Trousers with a tear
Old raffle tickets
Dad's smelly old ties
Poison to kill bats
Remains of our tent
A box of red mats
A dead, filthy mouse
Two smelly long socks
Jars of offered blood
A broken square box
A brand new football

Billy Hayes (9)
Woodthorpe Primary School

What's Up In The Attic?

You go to explore
When up attic steps
You'll find on the floor
These are the things
A karaoke mic
A green Christmas tree
An old broken bike
An electric car
A big box of buns
A weird box of toys
A set of old guns
A king-size, fat rat
Four smelly old socks
Seven smelly drawers
Loads of old boxes
A rusty Xbox
What's up in the attic?

Declan Horncastle (9)
Woodthorpe Primary School

Friends

Friends are good in every way.
They make today a special day.
They help when I'm feeling down.
We always walk together around town.
On birthdays they bring me a present.
And they are very, very pleasant.
We bring each other lots of toys.
At times we make a lot of noise.
We make each other laugh and scream.
Together we make a perfect team.
I really, really like my friends.
We hope our friendship never ends.

Chloe Fletcher (9)
Woodthorpe Primary School

What's Up In The Attic?

You go to explore
　When up the attic steps
　　You'll find on the floor
　　　These are the things
　　　　A funny old ted
　　　　　A broken old box
　　　　　　A creaky old bed
　　　　　　　Silly birthday cards
　　　　　　　　A broken old wagon
　　　　　　　　　Some broken old toys
　　　　　　　　　An old dragon
　　　　　　　　　　A broken dolls' house
　　　　　　　　　　　An old Christmas clock
　　　　　　　　　　　An old teddy bear
　　　　　　　　　　　　A smelly old sock
　　　　　　　　　　　　A popped old football

What's up in the attic?

Alex Fowler (10)
Woodthorpe Primary School

Autumn

Autumn is freezing cold.
Autumn is when leaves turn different colours.
Autumn is when conkers fall off.
Autumn is when animals get ready to hibernate.
Autumn is when leaves fall.
Autumn is when bare branches come.
Autumn is when splashing rain comes down.
Autumn is when squirrels collect acorns.
Autumn is when the bright sun shines in the sky.

Becky Muggeridge (7)
Woodthorpe Primary School

Up In The Attic

A big, big creature!
A scary red bull
A doll of a teacher
A broken TV
A rotten old pear
An old, smelly sock
A sticky, cobwebby chair
A shiny gold key
Two groovy clocks
One broken dolls' house
An old scruffy box
A flat beach ball
A big, black bat!
Two large boots
A hilarious hat
A squeaky
Small mouse.

Jessica Cheung (9)
Woodthorpe Primary School

My Best Friend Has Gone To Rome

My best friend has gone to Rome
She has already phoned home.

My best friend has a brother
And a very kind mother.

My best friend doesn't have too much to wear
And she really, really loves to eat pears.

My best friend is really kind
But she does not mind.

My best friend is my pleasure
She is my best friend forever.

Rebekah Moore (9)
Woodthorpe Primary School

Autumn

Autumn, changing colours of leaves,
Falling to the ground.
Brown conkers that people collect,
Falling from the trees.
Wrapped up in a warm, green coat,
Ready to be picked.
Wind blowing the leaves and conkers,
Squirrels gathering nuts and acorns.
Their autumn breath makes tiny clouds,
Whilst the leaves give the trees bare branches,
That are coloured green.
Orange, red, yellow and brown,
The ground gets wet from
The rain and hailstones.
Splashing rain making puddles,
No playing out, too wet for that.
Also the wind, the wind
Blows away your hat.
Bright sunshine means you cannot see in your car.

Thomas Ibbott (7)
Woodthorpe Primary School

Autumn

The leaves fall off the trees
The rain comes down
The birds go to find a warm place
The sky gets darker but the sun still comes out,
Sometimes!

Chelsea Richardson (7)
Woodthorpe Primary School

Autumn

Children playing games
Trees going bare
Sun's really low
School starting now
Collecting acorns, conkers red and brown
Leaves going orange, yellow
Animals hibernating
Plants dying
Very cold and windy
Splashing puddles
Leaves falling down
Eating ice cream
Going to beaches
Fish and chips
Crows come for corn
Birds lay eggs.

James Smith (7)
Woodthorpe Primary School

Autumn

Badgers digging,
Woodpeckers pecking,
Squirrels singing,
It's autumn, it's autumn,
Autumn you're the best.
But in each corner, behind each tree
Bugs are singing,
Slugs and snails dancing,
It's autumn, it's autumn,
Autumn, you're the best.

Lewis Fletcher (7)
Woodthorpe Primary School

What's Up In The Attic?

You go to explore
When up attic steps,
You'll find on the floor
These are the things
A little girl's dolls' house.
An old red train set.
A hairy grey mouse.
A big fat monkey.
A massive clock face.
A green, spiky tree
My ancient suitcase.
My little red bike.
An old wooden chest.
Lots of rusty toys.
My holey white vest.
A hairy spider.

What's up in the attic?

Keelie Mollan (9)
Woodthorpe Primary School

Dark Knight

Oh dark knight,
Spare us, please,
Don't boil our heads,
Burn our knees,
Take them, please,
Let me go free
And I will give some
Cheese!

Matthew Chaplin (9)
Woodthorpe Primary School

What's Up In The Attic?

Two crazy cats,
Christmas decorations,
Five flying bats,
A ripped-up painting,

And a green, mouldy flask,
A flicker of a bulb,
An African mask,
A set of torn cards

And a black, bouncing flea,
Three little mice,
And an old Christmas tree,
Some dirty plastic bottles,

An out-of-tune trombone,
Lots of dust,
A knotted old phone,
A broken TV.

What's up in the attic?

Amy Louise Martin (10)
Woodthorpe Primary School

Autumn

Autumn has lots of colours,
Leaves red and yellow with quite a lot of sun.
Leaves are dancing in the wind, singing,
Red, yellow.
It's autumn, hooray!

Evan Morris (7)
Woodthorpe Primary School

Autumn

Leaves are in disguise with colour,
Squirrels are gathering nuts,
Badgers are getting ready to hibernate,
It's always been that way.

Autumn, autumn, autumn,
Red, yellow and orange,
Autumn, autumn, autumn,
Halfway to paradise.

Green, juicy apples falling off the trees,
Bees are in their hives making honey,
Corn and wheat being ploughed.

Autumn, autumn, autumn,
Red, brown, gold,
That's what I've been told!

Jack Hughes (7)
Woodthorpe Primary School

Autumn

Bright, lonely plants getting blown away!
Scrunched-up leaves falling from the trees!
Splashing in the puddles!
Brown, empty bushes with nothing on!
Hailstones banging on the window!
Red trees with fallen branches
Birds sleeping in their nests
Yellow leaves on the tall trees
Conkers falling off red trees
Reading orange autumn books, drawing autumn pictures
Watching autumn videos
Squirrels gathering their nuts
Bright, early sunshine waking up
Colours of autumn are orange, red, yellow and brown.

Georgia Muir (7)
Woodthorpe Primary School

Dear Santa

I know I haven't been good
when I said I would.
I know I gave Reece two big fists,
and then sold my sister.
I know I stole Tom's bike,
then I pushed Mike.
I snuck some chocolate cake,
and then was sick on Jake.
I ran out of class,
gave Miss Hanman a moustache!
I didn't do my work,
called the head teacher a burk, (well he is).
I promise not to do that,
I promise every year,
but now I really mean it,
and I won't ever do it again, ever
But maybe, next year!

Emily Henman (10)
Woodthorpe Primary School

Some Mums

Some mums say, 'You're very good.'
Some mums say, 'Do this and that.'
Some mums say, 'How was school?'
Some mums say, 'Feed the cat.'

Some mums think you're a sweetheart.
Some mums think you're never a pain.
Some mums think you're gorgeous.
Some mums think you're driving me insane!

Rebecca Jakes (8)
Woodthorpe Primary School

What's Up In the Attic

You go to explore
When up attic steps
You'll find on the floor
These are the things
A sleeping dog
A set of old stuff
Dissected frogs
An ancient wooden box
Box of Scalectrix
A red and dead rat
A tarnished TV
A rusty set of hooks
A cracked OHP
Old, red shredded books
Traditional drums

What's up in the attic?

Benjamin Lacey (9)
Woodthorpe Primary School

What's Up In The Attic?

You go to explore
When up attic steps
You'll find on the floor
These are the things
Poison to kill mites
Remains of our tent
A box of old bits
A red, feathery plant
An old piece of ham
One long, smelly sock
Two jars of red jam
A broken, square tyre

What's up in the attic?

Amy Milne (9)
Woodthorpe Primary School

What's Up In The Attic?

You go to explore
When up attic steps
You'll find on the floor
These are the things
Except all the mice
I like it a lot
All dull but very nice
A boxed Christmas tree
Some old, tatty books
And some rusty dolls
Some decaying books
A demolished tent
And broken toy boats
All worn and dusty
A bag of old coats

What's up in the attic?

Charley Preston (9)
Woodthorpe Primary School

Opening And Closing Of The Classroom

The sprinting door swings open
Chairs get to the tables
Opening windows get a shock
Dancing pens spit words out on the paper
Books say their last stories
Chairs climb back on tables
Computers take their last look around the classroom before
shutting down
The door locks himself up and says goodnight to the quiet classroom.

Jordan Smith (10)
Woodthorpe Primary School

Stairs Poem

You go to explore
When up the attic steps
You'll find on the floor
These are the things
A non-working train
An old rusty pram
A broken TV
A smashed jar of jam
Some pongy dead cats
A white Christmas tree
Dead, brown smelly rats
A mashed red suitcase
An old pellet gun
A very damp box
A model aeroplane
Two kitchen clocks.

What's up in the attic?

Adam Saun (9)
Woodthorpe Primary School

Morning Comes

As the moon waves goodbye to one side of the world,
The sun remembers it's his time to shine.
As the stars fall asleep the sun winks, goodbye.
When the night sky gallops away the blue sky shines like crystal.
The mountains look down at their green, glorious palace.
As the river listens to the fish swimming away, it reminds him
that he is a king.
Trees try to grab back their leaves, like children catching
dandelion seeds.
A stone remembers it used to part of a king.

Harry Ford (10)
Woodthorpe Primary School

What's Up In The Attic?

You go to explore
    When up attic steps
        You'll find on the floor
            These are the things
                A man called Freddy
                    Unfun, disliked toys
                        Out of use teddies
                            Some horrid spiders
                                A doll of two boys
                                  A rubbish old box
                                    Out of fashion toys
                                      A cracked, weak floorboard
                                        Some old people's tools
                                          An ancient big key
                                            A scary, dead mouse

What's up in the attic?

Dylan Howlett (9)
Woodthorpe Primary School

Monday Morning

The computer woke up and turned itself on.
All of the tables leaped across the class quickly into their positions.
Thousands of books zoomed into their baskets and rested.
Chairs jumped slowly around the classroom into their places.
Mr Whiteboard washed his sparkly face, waiting to be used.
The jolly school woke up and opened its massive wide mouth.
The children came in like a herd of elephants.

Jamal Ahmed (10)
Woodthorpe Primary School

What's Up In The Attic?

A creaky old floor
An old train set
A knock at the door
A ghost, I bet
Mouldy old box
Smashed rotten cars
Battered old clocks
Small rotting jar
A Hallowe'en toe
A smashed TV
A ball that you throw
An old PE kit
A long smelly sock
An old piece of ham
A wooden red block
Three jars of jam
An old train set
A ghost, I bet

What's up in the attic?

Emily Smith (9)
Woodthorpe Primary School

The Good Old Rainbow

Black is a sad moment in my life
Yellow is the sun shining brightly in the sky
Red is a heart pumping away in my body
Green is the tree swaying in the wind
Blue is the sea crashing against the rocks
Purple is a grape that I am going to eat
Orange is a cold drink I like

I really like the rainbow.

Benjamin Acey (10)
Woodthorpe Primary School

What's Up In The Attic?

A broken blackboard
A piece of sharp cord
A big, brown violin
A dusty, mucky floor
A dusty old book
A sticky blob of jam
Near a rusty old box
A little, shiny key
And a big, black bug
A little grey rat
A mucky old rug
A broken TV
A big, black bat
Two large boots
A hilarious hat
A squeaky, small mouse.

Danielle Hickman (9)
Woodthorpe Primary School

George

I have a dog
His name is George.
He's a golden retriever
With very large paws.
He plays with sticks
He plays with balls
He's very fast
When he runs after them all.
When it's raining
He gets wet
Then comes home
To a nice, warm bed.

Chloe Richardson (8)
Woodthorpe Primary School

My Birthday List

I want,

A pink bike,
A purple kite,

A fashion book
A rubber duck,

A sports car
An electric guitar,

A trip to Rome,
A brand new home,

Away from my brother,
Away from my mother,

A blue laptop,
To say *stop!*

I want everything!

Stephanie Watmough (10)
Woodthorpe Primary School

Nature

The sun, orange and glossy, winks at the moon,
The moon, cheesy and bright, takes the stars with him to the other
side of the world,
The mountain rock looks down on his kingdom,
A flock of birds fly like an aeroplane over the sea,
The sea, fierce as a lion, swirls round and round,
Fish, gold and shiny, swim under the water.

Luke Wilson (10)
Woodthorpe Primary School

What You Shouldn't Do

When a teacher comes up to you,
Don't ask what to do.
When a bully asks your name,
Don't play his game.

When a big boy comes up to you
And tells you what to do,
Don't argue.

When you show your sister a spider,
Don't ask her for a fiver,
When a robber comes up to you,
Don't ask him to kill you.

When your sister's being approached by a bear,
Don't go back there.

When you go to the fair,
Don't ask for a free teddy bear.

James Chapman & Mapalo (8)
Woodthorpe Primary School

The World

The glistening moon awakes with the stars
As they flash to the bottom of the Earth.
The sun, warm and bright, winks to the moon, goodbye!
The sky dazzles away its dreams for morning to begin,
The birds sing the early morning song.
The gleaming mountain looks down at his golden kingdom,
The trees wave their long green hair,
The fish swim around the pond to awaken themselves.

Lauren Stewart (10)
Woodthorpe Primary School

Friday 15.20pm

The whiteboard switched off as the children left the room
The tap tuned off to save some water
The book closed and went into my tray
The children's work clung to the wall
The dictionary sat back on the shelf
One of the pictures fell asleep quickly
The computer switched itself off by flashing
All the chairs climbed onto the tables
The pencils wriggled in their trays quietly
My red planner put all the notes on it
The lights flickered off and finally went to sleep
The pictures of the war had a fight
Microbes wriggled round the classroom as Mrs Young left!

Hannah Brown (10)
Woodthorpe Primary School

Green

Green is a leaf,
growing on a bush.

Green is a Christmas
tree, standing in the corner,
decorated with twinkling lights.

Green is my wellies, used to
splash around in the mud.

Green is a leprechaun counting
clovers, sitting on a log.

Green is my bed, all cosy
warm.

Green is a tree frog sticking
to a tree, catching flies.

Green is a colour you'll find
lots of in my garden, in fact
it's my favourite colour.

Anna Sibley (10)
Woodthorpe Primary School

Blue

Blue is the sky
With its white, fluffy clouds.

Blue is the sea
Glowing brightly in the sun.

Blue is a whale
Coming up for fresh air.

Blue is a blueberry
Succulent and juicy.

Blue is a blue tit
Flying gracefully through the sky.

Blue is a kingfisher
With its glimmering, orange breast.

Joseph Devonport (10)
Woodthorpe Primary School

Pink

Pink is a girlie colour
Pink is my feather boa
Pink is the tulips in the field
Pink is the roses in an enchanted garden
Pink is Piglet from Winnie the Pooh
Pink is my mum made swimming bag
Pink is my bedroom, it's like a girlie-girl grotto
Pink is my school backpack
Pink is my pack-up
As you can see, my world is full of pink,
Pink and more pink!

Vicki Hall (10)
Woodthorpe Primary School

Red

Red is the fire
in the warm fireplace

Red is a love heart
for people in love

Red is ruby shining
on someone's finger

Red is a poppy
swaying in a field

Red is a rosy apple
getting ready to be bitten

Red is a red ball
played with by a kitten

Red is a Coca-Cola
wrapper on one of the bottles

Red is red wine
that makes people tipsy

Jennifer Tompkins (10)
Woodthorpe Primary School

Yellow

Yellow is the sun
Burning in the sky

Yellow is dandelions and daffodils
In my garden

Yellow is the sand
Made into sandcastles by children

Yellow is vanilla ice cream
With a flake stuck into it

Yellow is some ducklings
Lined up in single file behind their mum, swimming.

Zulfa Motin (10)
Woodthorpe Primary School

The Things Of The World

The boiling, golden sun winks to the
moon, as she walks away into the clouds

The glittery stars run after the moon as
if she were their mother

The sky unrolls her blue hair looking
down at land and sea

The sea covers the land like a soft
silk blanket

The giant, gravel mountain peers down at
his green kingdom

The electric-blue river flows down the
mountain valley as he is remembering to come back

The neon orange clownfish swims through
the ice-blue ocean

The brown chirping hedge sparrow flies in
the air like a jet-car

The thick, leafy trees nod their head for
another day is coming

The lonely stone looks at the big mountain,
knowing he used to be one.

David Bracknell (10)
Woodthorpe Primary School

In The Morning

The moon reminds herself of her dreams as she waves goodbye,
The golden sun waves to the moon and starts her day-shift.
All the stars follow the bright moon as she sails away
                                        for another night.
The sky is as blue as the morning sea,
Mountains look down on their flowery kingdoms.
Clear blue rivers rush through the long green grass,
The trees wave their long green hair in the morning breeze.

Jasmine Corley (10)
Woodthorpe Primary School

What's Up In The Attic?

A big spider
A barrel of cider
Two ancient mummies
And a box of dummies
A zombiefied fish
A china dish
Some broken glass
And a dead, grey ass
Some smelly rats
Two dead bats
A damp cigar
And a racing car
Some cobwebby boots
And a old-fashioned flute
My dad's old bike
His hamster called Spike
Some tubes of Smarties
And some hats for parties.

Pierce Carrington (9)
Woodthorpe Primary School

What Is Red?

Flames rising from the fire
Blood from a human body
The sky at the beginning of the day
The Devil rising from Hell
Lava pouring from a volcano
Anger letting its fury loose
A rose, just blooming.

Jack Liddle (11)
Woodthorpe Primary School

My Blue Poem

Blue is the clouds
Sheltering the sky.

Blue is a blueberry
That hangs on a bush.

Blue is water
Like the ocean.

Blue is a car
That rides on the road.
Blue is a house
That you live in.

Blue is a bedroom
That you sleep in.

Blue is a television
That you watch.

James Powell (10)
Woodthorpe Primary School

Things Of The World

The boiling golden sun winks to the moon
as she walks away into the clouds.
The glittery stars run after the moon
as if she is their mother.
The sky unrolls her blue hair
looking down at land and sea.
The giant, grand mountain peers down
at his green kingdom.
The electric-blue river flows down the mountain valley
as he is remembering to come back.
The neon orange clownfish
scutters through the ice-blue ocean.

Daniel Cliff (10)
Woodthorpe Primary School

Friday 3.20pm

The projector spied on the interactive whiteboard.
The pen raced across the paper to get to the tray.
The brown chairs jumped up in surprise at having no weight.
The plughole swallowed the clean, dripping water as it reached
the bowl.
The brown, plastic chairs climbed onto the tables for a good rest.
The classroom sighed with great relief.
The classroom cheered loudly as the children headed home
for the weekend!

Jasmine Corley (10)
Woodthorpe Primary School

Blue

Blue is the sky looking down on you and me
Blue are the eyes of my new baby brother
Blue is the colour of the babbling stream
Flowing through the woods and fields
Finding its way to the rivers and seas
Blue is the colour of the big blue whale
Swimming in the deep blue sea
Blue is the colour of bluebells in the spring
And of my mum's favourite blue vase.

Ryan Baines (10)
Woodthorpe Primary School